If you were me and lived in...
ISRAEL

A Child's Introduction to Culture Around the World

Carole P. Roman
Illustrated by Kelsea Wierenga

For David- who showed me the land and people of Israel
the way no one else could have.

Special thanks to Manya who will get a tickle seeing
her name here. Your encouragement and support mean
more than you know!

ISBN: 1537261991

ISBN 13: 978-1537261997

JERUSALEM

ISRAEL

If you were me and lived in Israel (Yiz-ra-el), you would call it the State of Israel or Medinat Israel (Me-din-at Iz-ra-el). Your home would be located in the Middle East on the southwestern shore of the Mediterranean (Med-it-ter-rain-ee-n) Sea.

Judaism (Jud-ee-is-em), Christianity (Chris-tee-an-it-ee), Islam (Is-lam), and the Baha'i (Bah-hay) faiths consider Israel as a Holy (Ho-lee) Land.

You might live in Jerusalem (Yer-rosh-a-lay-um). It is one of the oldest cities in the world with a long and interesting history.

In 1538 AD, Suleiman (Sul-i-man) the Magnificent, a Turkish king, built a wall around the old city. It is divided into four neighborhoods known as the Christian (Christ-een), Armenian (Ar-meen-ean), Muslim (Mus-lim), and Jewish (Jew-ish) quarters. Each group has ancient and important buildings in their section that brings millions of tourists to the city every year to learn and celebrate their religions.

Your name might be Noah (No-wah), Yonaton (Yon-a-ton), or Yosef (Yo-sef) if you are a boy. Your parents might have chosen Talia (Tal-ya), Maya (Mai-ya), or Shira (Shee-ra) if you are a girl.

When you call for Mommy, you would say Ima (EEm-a). Your daddy would respond to Abba (Ab-bah).

You love to go shopping with Ima and Abba in the shouk (shook), which is an open-air market filled with everything from clothing to assorted products and foods. You will go there to buy fresh hallav (ha-lav) and lechem (lech-em). Halav is milk, and lechem is bread. Abba always brings enough shekels (shek-els) to purchase groceries. The shekel originally meant "weighing" in the olden days when people traded wheat for other goods. People from many nations used different coins called shekels thousands of years ago. Israel decided to bring back the name of the ancient currency.

When you have visitors, you would insist they take a trip to the Dead Sea. It is the lowest spot in earth that can be reached by a car or bus. It is 1371 feet below sea level. It is also called the Salt Sea. People call it the Dead Sea because you won't find a fish or another living thing in it.

The water is too salty, and nothing can survive in it. It is a well known spa, and many people travel there to soak in the water to make them feel better.

Afterward, you travel to Tsaba (Za-ba) and Tzafta's (Zaf-ta's) house in Tel Aviv (Tel A-viv), which is an important city in Israel. Your grandparents' table will be filled with lots of fresh salads. Tzafta would make a mountain of falafel (fa-laf-el). She would fry the ground chickpeas into crunchy and flavorful balls. She tucks them into a round bread called a pita (pee-ta), adds lots of fresh tomatoes, cucumbers, and parsley, and tops it with tahini (ta-hin-ee) sauce. Tahini is ground sesame paste that you love to use for dipping. There will be a plate of shwarma (shwar-ma) and shnitzel (shnit-zel). Shwarma is grilled meat, usually turkey or lamb that is thinly shaved off a huge loaf. Shnitzel is delicate cutlets that she spent the morning frying to a crispy brown. Humus (Hum-us) will also be on the table as a dip for the meat. You love the mashed chickpea paste and can eat it for breakfast, lunch, or dinner.

For dessert, you love to eat honey-drenched baklava (bak-lav-a) that Zafta makes every Friday. Its flaky pastry is filled with dried fruits and chopped nuts that will melt in your mouth. You might enjoy eating a fistful of roasted fistookeim (fist-took-eam) or pistachios that are grown in Israel. You always finish the meal with juicy arbus (arbus). The tasty watermelon is a sweet treat.

14

You watch football matches on television. When you visit your cousins in the United States, you remember to call it soccer, as they do. You play outside with your friends when you aren't practicing track and field activities. You work hard to get into the Maccabiah (Mac-ca-bee-ya) Games. They are international contests similar to the Olympics (O-limp-pics) that are held every four years in Israel to find the best athletes.

Of course, you enjoy practicing Krav Maga (Krav Ma-gah) with your brother. You have taken lessons in Israeli (Is-rae-lee) special self-defense martial arts since you were little.

Your little sister will watch you and imitate your moves with her buba (bub-ah).

Afterward, you will go for glida (glee-dah). Can you guess what that is?

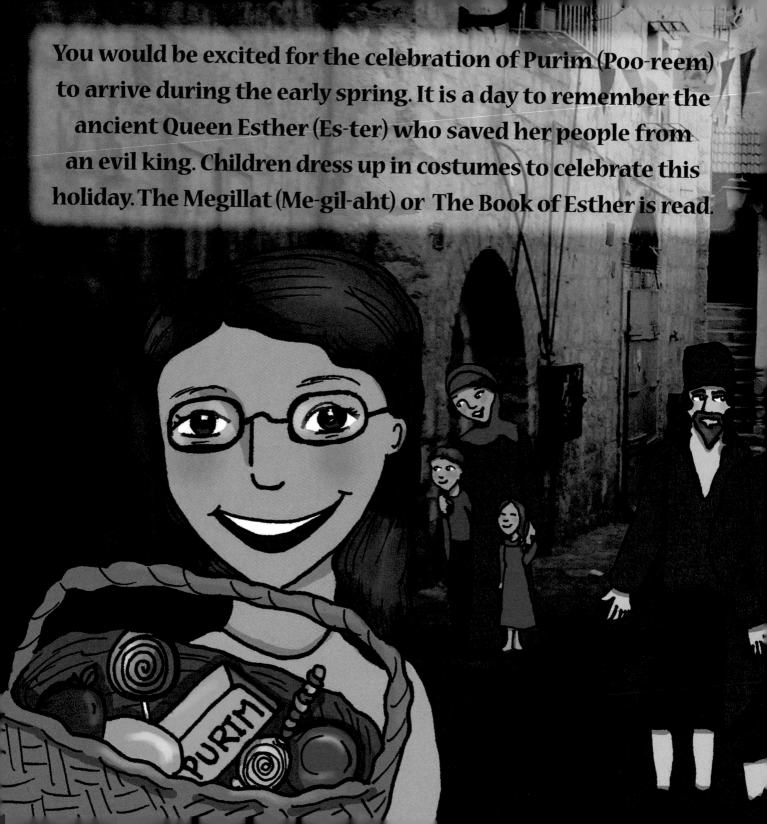

You would be excited for the celebration of Purim (Poo-reem) to arrive during the early spring. It is a day to remember the ancient Queen Esther (Es-ter) who saved her people from an evil king. Children dress up in costumes to celebrate this holiday. The Megillat (Me-gil-aht) or The Book of Esther is read.

There will be a delicious dinner. Charity is given to the poor, and special baskets filled with candy and treats are given to friends and relatives. There are parades, and when the evil king's name is mentioned, everybody uses a special noisemaker so you can't hear it.

In Israel, you might wonder why you read and write from the right side of the paper to the left when the rest of the world does it the other way around. Well, you would learn that in ancient times people used stone tablets instead of paper to write things down. They had to carve the surface of the stone using a hammer and chisel. The writer had to hold the hammer in his stronger hand, which was usually his right one so that he could make an impression on the rock. It was easier to go from the right to the left!

You will learn all about both ancient and modern Israel in biet safer (bey-et saf-fer) or the house of books. Can you figure why that is the word for school?

So you see, if you were me, how life in Israel could really be.

Pronunciation Guide

Abba (Ab-bah)- Daddy.

arbus (ar-bus)- watermelon.

Armenian (Ar-mee-nee-yun)- those following the Armenian church.

Bahai'I (Bah-ha-ee)- the Bahai'I faith.

baklava (bak-la-va)- a flaky pastry filled dried fruits and nuts.

biet safer (bey-et saf-fer)- a school.

buba (bub-ah)- a doll.

Christian (Cris--chan)- those following the Christian faith.

Christianity (Cris--tee-ann-i-tee)- the Christian faith.

Esther (Es-ter)- a Jewish queen who saved her people from an evil king.

falafel (fa-laf-el)- crunchy fried balls of ground chickpeas.

fistookeim (fist-took-eam)- pistachio nuts.

glida (glee-dah)- ice cream.

hallav (ha-lav)- milk.

Holy (Ho-lee) Land- several faiths hold places in Israel as important to their beliefs and history.

humas (hum-us)- mashed chickpeas used at every meal.

Ima (EEm-a)- Mommy.

Islam (Is-lam)- the Muslim faith.

Israel (Yiz-ra-el)- the State of Israel located in the Middle East.

Israeli (Is-rae-lee)- a person who was born in Israel.

Jewish (Jew-ish)- those following the Jewish faith.

Judaism (Ju-dee-is-em)- the Jewish faith.

Jerusalem (Ji-rooze-suh-lum)- the unrecognized capital of Israel.

Krav Maga (Krav Ma-gah)- an Israeli form of martial arts.

lechem (lech-am)- bread.

Maccabiah (Mac-ca-bee-yah) Games- the competitions that take place every four years to find the greatest athletes.

Maya (My-yah)- a popular girl's name in Israel.

Medinat Israel (Me-din-at Yiz-ra-el)- the official name for the State of Israel.

Mediterranean (Med-it-ter-rain-ee-an) Sea- the sea below Southern Europe and North of Israel.

Megillat (Me-gil-aht)- the book or story of Queen Esther from the Bible.

Muslim (Mus-lum)- those following the teaching of Islam.

Noah (No-wah)- a popular boy's name in Israel.

Olympics (Oh-lim-pics)- the competitions that take place every four years where the world's great athletes compete to see who is the best.

pita (pee-ta)- round pocket bread.

Purim (Poo-reem)- a holiday celebrating Queen Esther's bravery against an evil king.

shekels (shek-els)- the currency used in Israel.

shwarma (sh-war-ma)- grilled meats, usually lamb or turkey.

Shira (Shee-ra)- a popular girl's name in Israel.

shouk (shook)- the market.

shnitzel (shnit-zel)- pounded and fried cutlets, usually chicken.

spa (spa)- a business offering health and beauty treatments through such means as steam baths, exercise equipment, and massage.

Suleiman (Sul-i-man) the Magnificent- the leader of the Turkish Empire who built a wall around Jerusalem in 1538 AD.

Talia (Tal-ya)- a popular girl's name in Israel.

tahini (ta-hee-nee)- a grounded sesame paste used as a topping.

Tel Aviv (Tel Ah-viv)- the bustling city in Israel.

Tzafta (Zaf-ta)- Grandmother.

Tsaba (Za-ba)- Grandfather.

Yonaton (Yon-a-ton)- a popular boy's name in Israel.

Yosef (Yo-sef)- a popular boy's name in Israel.